XOXO
SPIRIT &
SOUL

SET IN SOUL

THIS JOURNAL BELONGS TO

_____

DEDICATED TO THE LIGHT
WITHIN US LOOKING FOR A
PLACE TO FREELY SHINE

TABLE OF CONTENTS

HOW TO USE THIS JOURNAL

XOXO Spirit & Soul is designed to provide spiritual love which leads to you operating at your best. One's spiritual journey is filled with twists and turns as well as ups and downs and it is because of this that it is easy for us to wonder if we are on the right path. You start to question if you are making the best decisions, if you are moving forward or remaining stagnant, how you can move forward and how to do that when you don't understand what is going on around you. You may even wonder when you will experience your next miracle because it may feel to you that it is way overdue. In the questioning of your spiritual journey, you may start to lose faith, experience doubt and lose confidence. XOXO Spirit & Soul is a journal that helps put things back into perspective. With this journal, you will gain clarity, insight, peace, acceptance, forgiveness as well as expect wellness and breakthroughs. This journal is a Christian based journal that should be used as an aid with other spiritual practices that you may already practice.

It is recommended to use this journal daily. It is with your handwritten words that you will start to see and understand what your spirit is saying. Put on the page what is in your heart. Be truthful and transparent. You will find that as you continue to do this, you will start to get stronger. You will know exactly your spirit needs. You will also find a new love with the life you are truly living. You will start to view yourself as close to how God views you. You deserve better. You deserve peace. You deserve to be proud of your spiritual walk because it is in your journey you will learn that God never left you. You are not alone and never will be. So, in your happy times, write. In your tough times, write. It is through your writing that you are communicating with yourself and most importantly God. Whatever you can't say out loud, write it down. This is your place to be vulnerable and everything your truly are.

May God Bless You Inside & Out.

XOXO Spirit & Soul

REFERENCE TO

OWNING YOUR PRESENT MOMENT

I Believe:

I Believe God Will:

My Favorite Prayer:

I Want To Heal From:

OWNING YOUR PRESENT MOMENT

I Want Forgiveness From:

I Want To Forgive:

I Need Restoration In:

I Want To Grow In:

What Has Always Stuck With Me:

OWNING YOUR PRESENT MOMENT

It Has Always Been Difficult For Me To:

The Last Miracle That Changed My Life:

The Breakthrough That I Need Right Now:

I Will Finally Let Go Of:

I'm Making Room For:

OWNING YOUR PRESENT MOMENT

I Believe God:

What I Know About God:

How God Makes Me Smile:

The Most Recent Gift God Gave Me:

If God Forgave Me, Then I:

OWNING YOUR PRESENT MOMENT

Everyday I Need:

If It Wasn't For God, I:

Because Of God I:

My Relationship With God:

Everyday I Ask:

OWNING YOUR PRESENT MOMENT

Everyday I Plan To Grow My Relationship With The Most High By:

What I Am Trying To Understand Right Now:

In My Scared Space I:

Are You Open To God's Signs?

Do You Believe You Are Currently On The Right Path In Life?

OWNING YOUR PRESENT MOMENT

My Sacred Space With God Is:

I Trust My _____In The Hands Of God.

Short Term Request:

Long Term Request:

SECTION ONE

SEEDED IN THE WORD: FAITH AND FORGIVENESS

FAITH AND FORGIVENESS

Today: Mood:

Today I Am Grateful For: Today's Scripture I Will Meditate On:

Today's Prayer: What This Scripture Means To Me:

Today I Pray For (Name The Person Who   I Forgive These People:
You Pray For And What The Prayer Is
Towards):

Today I Believe God Is Asking Me: Today I Will Let Go Of:

Today I Am Open To: Today I Free Myself From:

Today I Forgive Myself For: I Know That The Blood Of Christ:

By The Grace Of God I Am: I Have Faith That:

FAITH AND FORGIVENESS

Today: Mood:

Today I Am Grateful For: Today's Scripture I Will Meditate On:

Today's Prayer: What This Scripture Means To Me:

Today I Pray For (Name The Person Who   I Forgive These People:
You Pray For And What The Prayer Is
Towards):

Today I Believe God Is Asking Me: Today I Will Let Go Of:

Today I Am Open To: Today I Free Myself From:

Today I Forgive Myself For: I Know That The Blood Of Christ:

By The Grace Of God I Am: I Have Faith That:

FAITH AND FORGIVENESS

Today: Mood:

Today I Am Grateful For: Today's Scripture I Will Meditate On:

Today's Prayer: What This Scripture Means To Me:

Today I Pray For (Name The Person Who   I Forgive These People:
You Pray For And What The Prayer Is
Towards):

Today I Believe God Is Asking Me: Today I Will Let Go Of:

Today I Am Open To: Today I Free Myself From:

Today I Forgive Myself For: I Know That The Blood Of Christ:

By The Grace Of God I Am: I Have Faith That:

A FORGIVENESS LETTER TO MYSELF

FAITH AND FORGIVENESS

Today: Mood:

Today I Am Grateful For: Today's Scripture I Will Meditate On:

Today's Prayer: What This Scripture Means To Me:

Today I Pray For (Name The Person Who   I Forgive These People:
You Pray For And What The Prayer Is
Towards):

Today I Believe God Is Asking Me: Today I Will Let Go Of:

Today I Am Open To: Today I Free Myself From:

Today I Forgive Myself For: I Know That The Blood Of Christ:

By The Grace Of God I Am: I Have Faith That:

21

But you, O Lord, are a compassionate and gracious God, slow to anger, abounding in love and faithfulness. Psalm 86:15

FAITH AND FORGIVENESS

Today:

Mood:

Today I Am Grateful For:

Today's Scripture I Will Meditate On:

Today's Prayer:

What This Scripture Means To Me:

Today I Pray For (Name The Person Who You Pray For And What The Prayer Is Towards):

I Forgive These People:

Today I Believe God Is Asking Me:

Today I Will Let Go Of:

Today I Am Open To:

Today I Free Myself From:

Today I Forgive Myself For:

I Know That The Blood Of Christ:

By The Grace Of God I Am:

I Have Faith That:

FAITH AND FORGIVENESS

Today: Mood:

Today I Am Grateful For: Today's Scripture I Will Meditate On:

Today's Prayer: What This Scripture Means To Me:

Today I Pray For (Name The Person Who   I Forgive These People.
You Pray For And What The Prayer Is
Towards):

Today I Believe God Is Asking Me: Today I Will Let Go Of:

Today I Am Open To: Today I Free Myself From:

Today I Forgive Myself For: I Know That The Blood Of Christ:

By The Grace Of God I Am: I Have Faith That:

Let all that you do be done in love. 1 Corinthians 16:14

I FORGAVE...
THEN
I let it go.

FAITH AND FORGIVENESS

Today:

Mood:

Today I Am Grateful For:

Today's Scripture I Will Meditate On:

Today's Prayer:

What This Scripture Means To Me:

Today I Pray For (Name The Person Who You Pray For And What The Prayer Is Towards):

I Forgive These People:

Today I Believe God Is Asking Me:

Today I Will Let Go Of:

Today I Am Open To:

Today I Free Myself From:

Today I Forgive Myself For:

I Know That The Blood Of Christ:

By The Grace Of God I Am:

I Have Faith That:

Be still, and know that I am God. I will be exalted among the nations, I will be exalted in the earth! Psalm 46:10

FAITH AND FORGIVENESS

Today:

Mood:

Today I Am Grateful For:

Today's Scripture I Will Meditate On:

Today's Prayer:

What This Scripture Means To Me:

Today I Pray For (Name The Person Who You Pray For And What The Prayer Is Towards):

I Forgive These People:

Today I Believe God Is Asking Me:

Today I Will Let Go Of:

Today I Am Open To:

Today I Free Myself From:

Today I Forgive Myself For:

I Know That The Blood Of Christ:

By The Grace Of God I Am:

I Have Faith That:

FAITH AND FORGIVENESS

Today: Mood:

Today I Am Grateful For: Today's Scripture I Will Meditate On:

Today's Prayer: What This Scripture Means To Me:

Today I Pray For (Name The Person Who   I Forgive These People:
You Pray For And What The Prayer Is
Towards):

Today I Believe God Is Asking Me: Today I Will Let Go Of:

Today I Am Open To: Today I Free Myself From:

Today I Forgive Myself For: I Know That The Blood Of Christ:

By The Grace Of God I Am: I Have Faith That:

Your word is a lamp for my feet, a light on my path. Psalm 119:105

FAITH AND FORGIVENESS

Today: Mood:

Today I Am Grateful For: Today's Scripture I Will Meditate On:

Today's Prayer: What This Scripture Means To Me:

Today I Pray For (Name The Person Who   I Forgive These People:
You Pray For And What The Prayer Is
Towards):

Today I Believe God Is Asking Me: Today I Will Let Go Of:

Today I Am Open To: Today I Free Myself From:

Today I Forgive Myself For: I Know That The Blood Of Christ:

By The Grace Of God I Am: I Have Faith That:

ONCE I STARTED TO **FORGIVE,** That's When I Began To Win.

I Had Enough Faith To Realize

THAT WHAT I WAS
HOLDING ON TO WASN'T
WORTH

What Was Coming.
So I Dropped It And Forgave Myself.

FAITH AND FORGIVENESS

Today: Mood:

Today I Am Grateful For: Today's Scripture I Will Meditate On:

Today's Prayer: What This Scripture Means To Me:

Today I Pray For (Name The Person Who   I Forgive These People:
You Pray For And What The Prayer Is
Towards):

Today I Believe God Is Asking Me: Today I Will Let Go Of:

Today I Am Open To: Today I Free Myself From:

Today I Forgive Myself For: I Know That The Blood Of Christ:

By The Grace Of God I Am: I Have Faith That:

FAITH AND FORGIVENESS

Today: Mood:

Today I Am Grateful For: Today's Scripture I Will Meditate On:

Today's Prayer: What This Scripture Means To Me:

Today I Pray For (Name The Person Who   I Forgive These People:
You Pray For And What The Prayer Is
Towards):

Today I Believe God Is Asking Me: Today I Will Let Go Of:

Today I Am Open To: Today I Free Myself From:

Today I Forgive Myself For: I Know That The Blood Of Christ:

By The Grace Of God I Am: I Have Faith That:

FAITH AND FORGIVENESS

Today: Mood:

Today I Am Grateful For: Today's Scripture I Will Meditate On:

Today's Prayer: What This Scripture Means To Me:

Today I Pray For (Name The Person Who   I Forgive These People:
You Pray For And What The Prayer Is
Towards):

Today I Believe God Is Asking Me: Today I Will Let Go Of:

Today I Am Open To: Today I Free Myself From:

Today I Forgive Myself For: I Know That The Blood Of Christ:

By The Grace Of God I Am: I Have Faith That:

FAITH AND FORGIVENESS

Today: Mood:

Today I Am Grateful For: Today's Scripture I Will Meditate On:

Today's Prayer: What This Scripture Means To Me:

Today I Pray For (Name The Person Who   I Forgive These People:
You Pray For And What The Prayer Is
Towards):

Today I Believe God Is Asking Me: Today I Will Let Go Of:

Today I Am Open To: Today I Free Myself From:

Today I Forgive Myself For: I Know That The Blood Of Christ:

By The Grace Of God I Am: I Have Faith That:

FAITH AND FORGIVENESS

Today:

Mood:

Today I Am Grateful For:

Today's Scripture I Will Meditate On:

Today's Prayer:

What This Scripture Means To Me:

Today I Pray For (Name The Person Who You Pray For And What The Prayer Is Towards):

I Forgive These People:

Today I Believe God Is Asking Me:

Today I Will Let Go Of:

Today I Am Open To:

Today I Free Myself From:

Today I Forgive Myself For:

I Know That The Blood Of Christ:

By The Grace Of God I Am:

I Have Faith That:

A FORGIVENESS LETTER TO THE PERSON I HAD A HARD TIME FORGIVING

FAITH AND FORGIVENESS

Today: Mood:

Today I Am Grateful For: Today's Scripture I Will Meditate On:

Today's Prayer: What This Scripture Means To Me:

Today I Pray For (Name The Person Who   I Forgive These People.
You Pray For And What The Prayer Is
Towards):

Today I Believe God Is Asking Me: Today I Will Let Go Of:

Today I Am Open To: Today I Free Myself From:

Today I Forgive Myself For: I Know That The Blood Of Christ:

By The Grace Of God I Am: I Have Faith That:

SPIRITUAL ACTION:

TAKE TWENTY MINUTES TO PRESENT YOUR FEARS & WORRIES TO GOD. TAKE ANOTHER TWENTY MINUTES TO TELL GOD HOW GRATEFUL YOU ARE TO LET GO & HAND EACH & EVERY FEAR & WORRY TO HIM. END THIS ACTION BY REPEATING "I BELIEVE IT IS DONE."

PEACE
LEAVE WITH YOU;
my peace I give to you.

Not as the world gives do I give to you.
Let not your hearts be troubled, neither
let them be afraid.
John 14:27

FAITH AND FORGIVENESS

Today: Mood:

Today I Am Grateful For: Today's Scripture I Will Meditate On:

Today's Prayer: What This Scripture Means To Me:

Today I Pray For (Name The Person Who   I Forgive These People:
You Pray For And What The Prayer Is
Towards):

Today I Believe God Is Asking Me: Today I Will Let Go Of:

Today I Am Open To: Today I Free Myself From:

Today I Forgive Myself For: I Know That The Blood Of Christ:

By The Grace Of God I Am: I Have Faith That:

FAITH AND FORGIVENESS

Today: Mood:

Today I Am Grateful For: Today's Scripture I Will Meditate On:

Today's Prayer: What This Scripture Means To Me:

Today I Pray For (Name The Person Who   I Forgive These People:
You Pray For And What The Prayer Is
Towards):

Today I Believe God Is Asking Me: Today I Will Let Go Of:

Today I Am Open To: Today I Free Myself From:

Today I Forgive Myself For: I Know That The Blood Of Christ:

By The Grace Of God I Am: I Have Faith That:

FAITH AND FORGIVENESS

Today:

Mood:

Today I Am Grateful For:

Today's Scripture I Will Meditate On:

Today's Prayer:

What This Scripture Means To Me:

Today I Pray For (Name The Person Who You Pray For And What The Prayer Is Towards):

I Forgive These People:

Today I Believe God Is Asking Me:

Today I Will Let Go Of:

Today I Am Open To:

Today I Free Myself From:

Today I Forgive Myself For:

I Know That The Blood Of Christ:

By The Grace Of God I Am:

I Have Faith That:

YOUR
FAITH
Has Made You Well
- Jesus

FAITH AND FORGIVENESS

Today: Mood:

Today I Am Grateful For: Today's Scripture I Will Meditate On:

Today's Prayer: What This Scripture Means To Me:

Today I Pray For (Name The Person Who   I Forgive These People:
You Pray For And What The Prayer Is
Towards):

Today I Believe God Is Asking Me: Today I Will Let Go Of:

Today I Am Open To: Today I Free Myself From:

Today I Forgive Myself For: I Know That The Blood Of Christ:

By The Grace Of God I Am: I Have Faith That:

FAITH AND FORGIVENESS

Today:

Mood:

Today I Am Grateful For:

Today's Scripture I Will Meditate On:

Today's Prayer:

What This Scripture Means To Me:

Today I Pray For (Name The Person Who You Pray For And What The Prayer Is Towards):

I Forgive These People:

Today I Believe God Is Asking Me:

Today I Will Let Go Of:

Today I Am Open To:

Today I Free Myself From:

Today I Forgive Myself For:

I Know That The Blood Of Christ:

By The Grace Of God I Am:

I Have Faith That:

This is the confidence we have in approaching God: that if we ask anything according to his will, he hears us. 1 John 5:14

FAITH AND FORGIVENESS

Today: Mood:

Today I Am Grateful For: Today's Scripture I Will Meditate On:

Today's Prayer: What This Scripture Means To Me:

Today I Pray For (Name The Person Who   I Forgive These People:
You Pray For And What The Prayer Is
Towards):

Today I Believe God Is Asking Me: Today I Will Let Go Of:

Today I Am Open To: Today I Free Myself From:

Today I Forgive Myself For: I Know That The Blood Of Christ:

By The Grace Of God I Am: I Have Faith That:

WHEN
YOUR FAITH
Is Louder Than Your Mouth....

FAITH AND FORGIVENESS

Today: Mood:

Today I Am Grateful For: Today's Scripture I Will Meditate On:

Today's Prayer: What This Scripture Means To Me:

Today I Pray For (Name The Person Who   I Forgive These People:
You Pray For And What The Prayer Is
Towards):

Today I Believe God Is Asking Me: Today I Will Let Go Of:

Today I Am Open To: Today I Free Myself From:

Today I Forgive Myself For: I Know That The Blood Of Christ:

By The Grace Of God I Am: I Have Faith That:

FAITH AND FORGIVENESS

Today:

Mood:

Today I Am Grateful For:

Today's Scripture I Will Meditate On:

Today's Prayer:

What This Scripture Means To Me:

Today I Pray For (Name The Person Who You Pray For And What The Prayer Is Towards):

I Forgive These People.

Today I Believe God Is Asking Me:

Today I Will Let Go Of:

Today I Am Open To:

Today I Free Myself From:

Today I Forgive Myself For:

I Know That The Blood Of Christ:

By The Grace Of God I Am:

I Have Faith That:

I will lie down and sleep in peace, for you alone, O Lord, make me dwell in safety. Psalm 4:8

FAITH AND FORGIVENESS

Today: Mood:

Today I Am Grateful For: Today's Scripture I Will Meditate On:

Today's Prayer: What This Scripture Means To Me:

Today I Pray For (Name The Person Who   I Forgive These People:
You Pray For And What The Prayer Is
Towards):

Today I Believe God Is Asking Me: Today I Will Let Go Of:

Today I Am Open To: Today I Free Myself From:

Today I Forgive Myself For: I Know That The Blood Of Christ:

By The Grace Of God I Am: I Have Faith That:

TODAY'S LOVE NOTE
TO GOD

FAITH AND FORGIVENESS

Today: Mood:

Today I Am Grateful For: Today's Scripture I Will Meditate On:

Today's Prayer: What This Scripture Means To Me:

Today I Pray For (Name The Person Who   I Forgive These People:
You Pray For And What The Prayer Is
Towards):

Today I Believe God Is Asking Me: Today I Will Let Go Of:

Today I Am Open To: Today I Free Myself From:

Today I Forgive Myself For: I Know That The Blood Of Christ:

By The Grace Of God I Am: I Have Faith That:

52

FAITH AND FORGIVENESS

Today: Mood:

Today I Am Grateful For: Today's Scripture I Will Meditate On:

Today's Prayer: What This Scripture Means To Me:

Today I Pray For (Name The Person Who   I Forgive These People.
You Pray For And What The Prayer Is
Towards):

Today I Believe God Is Asking Me: Today I Will Let Go Of:

Today I Am Open To: Today I Free Myself From:

Today I Forgive Myself For: I Know That The Blood Of Christ:

By The Grace Of God I Am: I Have Faith That:

FAITH AND FORGIVENESS

Today:

Mood:

Today I Am Grateful For:

Today's Scripture I Will Meditate On:

Today's Prayer:

What This Scripture Means To Me:

Today I Pray For (Name The Person Who You Pray For And What The Prayer Is Towards):

I Forgive These People:

Today I Believe God Is Asking Me:

Today I Will Let Go Of:

Today I Am Open To:

Today I Free Myself From:

Today I Forgive Myself For:

I Know That The Blood Of Christ:

By The Grace Of God I Am:

I Have Faith That:

FAITH AND FORGIVENESS

Today: Mood:

Today I Am Grateful For: Today's Scripture I Will Meditate On:

Today's Prayer: What This Scripture Means To Me:

Today I Pray For (Name The Person Who   I Forgive These People.
You Pray For And What The Prayer Is
Towards):

Today I Believe God Is Asking Me: Today I Will Let Go Of:

Today I Am Open To: Today I Free Myself From:

Today I Forgive Myself For: I Know That The Blood Of Christ:

By The Grace Of God I Am: I Have Faith That:

FAITH AND FORGIVENESS

Today: Mood:

Today I Am Grateful For: Today's Scripture I Will Meditate On:

Today's Prayer: What This Scripture Means To Me:

Today I Pray For (Name The Person Who   I Forgive These People:
You Pray For And What The Prayer Is
Towards):

Today I Believe God Is Asking Me: Today I Will Let Go Of:

Today I Am Open To: Today I Free Myself From:

Today I Forgive Myself For: I Know That The Blood Of Christ:

By The Grace Of God I Am: I Have Faith That:

56

FAITH AND FORGIVENESS

Today: Mood:

Today I Am Grateful For:

Today's Scripture I Will Meditate On:

Today's Prayer:

What This Scripture Means To Me:

Today I Pray For (Name The Person Who You Pray For And What The Prayer Is Towards):

I Forgive These People:

Today I Believe God Is Asking Me:

Today I Will Let Go Of:

Today I Am Open To:

Today I Free Myself From:

Today I Forgive Myself For:

I Know That The Blood Of Christ:

By The Grace Of God I Am:

I Have Faith That:

MAY THE
GOD

of hope fill you with all joy and peace as you trust in him, so that you may overflow with hope by the power of the Holy Spirit. Romans 15:13

FAITH AND FORGIVENESS

Today: Mood:

Today I Am Grateful For: Today's Scripture I Will Meditate On:

Today's Prayer: What This Scripture Means To Me:

Today I Pray For (Name The Person Who   I Forgive These People.
You Pray For And What The Prayer Is
Towards):

Today I Believe God Is Asking Me: Today I Will Let Go Of:

Today I Am Open To: Today I Free Myself From:

Today I Forgive Myself For: I Know That The Blood Of Christ:

By The Grace Of God I Am: I Have Faith That:

FAITH AND FORGIVENESS

Today: Mood:

Today I Am Grateful For: Today's Scripture I Will Meditate On:

Today's Prayer: What This Scripture Means To Me:

Today I Pray For (Name The Person Who   I Forgive These People:
You Pray For And What The Prayer Is
Towards):

Today I Believe God Is Asking Me: Today I Will Let Go Of:

Today I Am Open To: Today I Free Myself From:

Today I Forgive Myself For: I Know That The Blood Of Christ:

By The Grace Of God I Am: I Have Faith That:

TELL
YOUR HEART
That It Will Be Beating Much
Faster Very Often Because You
Are Replacing Fear For Faith.

FAITH AND FORGIVENESS

Today: Mood:

Today I Am Grateful For: Today's Scripture I Will Meditate On:

Today's Prayer: What This Scripture Means To Me:

Today I Pray For (Name The Person Who   I Forgive These People:
You Pray For And What The Prayer Is
Towards):

Today I Believe God Is Asking Me: Today I Will Let Go Of:

Today I Am Open To: Today I Free Myself From:

Today I Forgive Myself For: I Know That The Blood Of Christ:

By The Grace Of God I Am: I Have Faith That:

FAITH AND FORGIVENESS

Today: Mood:

Today I Am Grateful For: Today's Scripture I Will Meditate On:

Today's Prayer: What This Scripture Means To Me:

Today I Pray For (Name The Person Who   I Forgive These People:
You Pray For And What The Prayer Is
Towards):

Today I Believe God Is Asking Me: Today I Will Let Go Of:

Today I Am Open To: Today I Free Myself From:

Today I Forgive Myself For: I Know That The Blood Of Christ:

By The Grace Of God I Am: I Have Faith That:

FAITH AND FORGIVENESS

Today: Mood:

Today I Am Grateful For: Today's Scripture I Will Meditate On:

Today's Prayer: What This Scripture Means To Me:

Today I Pray For (Name The Person Who   I Forgive These People:
You Pray For And What The Prayer Is
Towards):

Today I Believe God Is Asking Me: Today I Will Let Go Of:

Today I Am Open To: Today I Free Myself From:

Today I Forgive Myself For: I Know That The Blood Of Christ:

By The Grace Of God I Am: I Have Faith That:

YOUR
SACRIFICE

was always required to see how much you believed. You will be rewarded. Faith based work gets you faith based results.

FORGIVE
THE PAST.
REMEMBER THE LESSON.

FAITH AND FORGIVENESS

Today: | Mood:

Today I Am Grateful For: | Today's Scripture I Will Meditate On:

Today's Prayer: | What This Scripture Means To Me:

Today I Pray For (Name The Person Who You Pray For And What The Prayer Is Towards): | I Forgive These People:

Today I Believe God Is Asking Me: | Today I Will Let Go Of:

Today I Am Open To: | Today I Free Myself From:

Today I Forgive Myself For: | I Know That The Blood Of Christ:

By The Grace Of God I Am: | I Have Faith That:

FAITH AND FORGIVENESS

Today: Mood:

Today I Am Grateful For: Today's Scripture I Will Meditate On:

Today's Prayer: What This Scripture Means To Me:

Today I Pray For (Name The Person Who   I Forgive These People:
You Pray For And What The Prayer Is
Towards):

Today I Believe God Is Asking Me: Today I Will Let Go Of:

Today I Am Open To: Today I Free Myself From:

Today I Forgive Myself For: I Know That The Blood Of Christ:

By The Grace Of God I Am: I Have Faith That:

FAITH AND FORGIVENESS

Today: Mood:

Today I Am Grateful For: Today's Scripture I Will Meditate On:

Today's Prayer: What This Scripture Means To Me:

Today I Pray For (Name The Person Who   I Forgive These People:
You Pray For And What The Prayer Is
Towards):

Today I Believe God Is Asking Me: Today I Will Let Go Of:

Today I Am Open To: Today I Free Myself From:

Today I Forgive Myself For: I Know That The Blood Of Christ:

By The Grace Of God I Am: I Have Faith That:

For everyone born of God overcomes the world. This is the victory that has overcome the world, even our faith. 1 John 5:4

IT'S OKAY TO MAKE
MISTAKES
AND ASK FOR FORGIVENESS.

You Should Be Able To Also Forgive Yourself And Move Forward. What You Do Not Have To Accept Is Being Crucified For It. Forgive The Crucifier. Bless Them And Keep It Moving.

FAITH AND FORGIVENESS

Today: Mood:

Today I Am Grateful For: Today's Scripture I Will Meditate On:

Today's Prayer: What This Scripture Means To Me:

Today I Pray For (Name The Person Who   I Forgive These People:
You Pray For And What The Prayer Is
Towards):

Today I Believe God Is Asking Me: Today I Will Let Go Of:

Today I Am Open To: Today I Free Myself From:

Today I Forgive Myself For: I Know That The Blood Of Christ:

By The Grace Of God I Am: I Have Faith That:

FAITH AND FORGIVENESS

Today: Mood:

Today I Am Grateful For: Today's Scripture I Will Meditate On:

Today's Prayer: What This Scripture Means To Me:

Today I Pray For (Name The Person Who   I Forgive These People:
You Pray For And What The Prayer Is
Towards):

Today I Believe God Is Asking Me: Today I Will Let Go Of:

Today I Am Open To: Today I Free Myself From:

Today I Forgive Myself For: I Know That The Blood Of Christ:

By The Grace Of God I Am: I Have Faith That:

FAITH AND FORGIVENESS

Today: Mood:

Today I Am Grateful For: Today's Scripture I Will Meditate On:

Today's Prayer: What This Scripture Means To Me:

Today I Pray For (Name The Person Who   I Forgive These People:
You Pray For And What The Prayer Is
Towards):

Today I Believe God Is Asking Me: Today I Will Let Go Of:

Today I Am Open To: Today I Free Myself From:

Today I Forgive Myself For: I Know That The Blood Of Christ:

By The Grace Of God I Am: I Have Faith That:

I have chosen the way of faithfulness; I have set my heart on your laws. Psalm 119:30

IN MY SACRED SPACE I

FAITH AND FORGIVENESS

Today:

Mood:

Today I Am Grateful For:

Today's Scripture I Will Meditate On:

Today's Prayer:

What This Scripture Means To Me:

Today I Pray For (Name The Person Who You Pray For And What The Prayer Is Towards):

I Forgive These People:

Today I Believe God Is Asking Me:

Today I Will Let Go Of:

Today I Am Open To:

Today I Free Myself From:

Today I Forgive Myself For:

I Know That The Blood Of Christ:

By The Grace Of God I Am:

I Have Faith That:

FAITH AND FORGIVENESS

Today:

Mood:

Today I Am Grateful For:

Today's Scripture I Will Meditate On:

Today's Prayer:

What This Scripture Means To Me:

Today I Pray For (Name The Person Who You Pray For And What The Prayer Is Towards):

I Forgive These People:

Today I Believe God Is Asking Me:

Today I Will Let Go Of:

Today I Am Open To:

Today I Free Myself From:

Today I Forgive Myself For:

I Know That The Blood Of Christ:

By The Grace Of God I Am:

I Have Faith That:

FAITH AND FORGIVENESS

Today: Mood:

Today I Am Grateful For: Today's Scripture I Will Meditate On:

Today's Prayer: What This Scripture Means To Me:

Today I Pray For (Name The Person Who   I Forgive These People.
You Pray For And What The Prayer Is
Towards):

Today I Believe God Is Asking Me: Today I Will Let Go Of:

Today I Am Open To: Today I Free Myself From:

Today I Forgive Myself For: I Know That The Blood Of Christ:

By The Grace Of God I Am: I Have Faith That:

FAITH AND FORGIVENESS

Today: Mood:

Today I Am Grateful For: Today's Scripture I Will Meditate On:

Today's Prayer: What This Scripture Means To Me:

Today I Pray For (Name The Person Who   I Forgive These People:
You Pray For And What The Prayer Is
Towards):

Today I Believe God Is Asking Me: Today I Will Let Go Of:

Today I Am Open To: Today I Free Myself From:

Today I Forgive Myself For: I Know That The Blood Of Christ:

By The Grace Of God I Am: I Have Faith That:

I BELIEVE

TODAY
I WILL LAUGH.

Today I Will Only See
Good. Today I Will
Forgive.

FAITH AND FORGIVENESS

Today:

Mood:

Today I Am Grateful For:

Today's Scripture I Will Meditate On:

Today's Prayer:

What This Scripture Means To Me:

Today I Pray For (Name The Person Who You Pray For And What The Prayer Is Towards):

I Forgive These People.

Today I Believe God Is Asking Me:

Today I Will Let Go Of:

Today I Am Open To:

Today I Free Myself From:

Today I Forgive Myself For:

I Know That The Blood Of Christ:

By The Grace Of God I Am:

I Have Faith That:

FAITH AND FORGIVENESS

Today:

Mood:

Today I Am Grateful For:

Today's Scripture I Will Meditate On:

Today's Prayer:

What This Scripture Means To Me:

Today I Pray For (Name The Person Who You Pray For And What The Prayer Is Towards):

I Forgive These People:

Today I Believe God Is Asking Me:

Today I Will Let Go Of:

Today I Am Open To:

Today I Free Myself From:

Today I Forgive Myself For:

I Know That The Blood Of Christ:

By The Grace Of God I Am:

I Have Faith That:

FAITH AND FORGIVENESS

Today: Mood:

Today I Am Grateful For: Today's Scripture I Will Meditate On:

Today's Prayer: What This Scripture Means To Me:

Today I Pray For (Name The Person Who   I Forgive These People.
You Pray For And What The Prayer Is
Towards):

Today I Believe God Is Asking Me: Today I Will Let Go Of:

Today I Am Open To: Today I Free Myself From:

Today I Forgive Myself For: I Know That The Blood Of Christ:

By The Grace Of God I Am: I Have Faith That:

Cast all your anxiety on him because he cares for you. 1 Peter 5:7

WHILE
YOU ARE WAITING

On An Apology, God
Is Waiting On You To
Just Forgive. Get More
Without Expecting
Anything.

FAITH AND FORGIVENESS

Today: Mood:

Today I Am Grateful For: Today's Scripture I Will Meditate On:

Today's Prayer: What This Scripture Means To Me:

Today I Pray For (Name The Person Who   I Forgive These People:
You Pray For And What The Prayer Is
Towards):

Today I Believe God Is Asking Me: Today I Will Let Go Of:

Today I Am Open To: Today I Free Myself From:

Today I Forgive Myself For: I Know That The Blood Of Christ:

By The Grace Of God I Am: I Have Faith That:

The LORD is a refuge for the oppressed, a stronghold in times of trouble. Psalm 9:9

FAITH AND FORGIVENESS

Today: Mood:

Today I Am Grateful For: Today's Scripture I Will Meditate On:

Today's Prayer: What This Scripture Means To Me:

Today I Pray For (Name The Person Who   I Forgive These People:
You Pray For And What The Prayer Is
Towards):

Today I Believe God Is Asking Me: Today I Will Let Go Of:

Today I Am Open To: Today I Free Myself From:

Today I Forgive Myself For: I Know That The Blood Of Christ:

By The Grace Of God I Am: I Have Faith That:

And now these three remain: faith, hope and love. But the greatest of these is love. 1 Corinthians 13:13

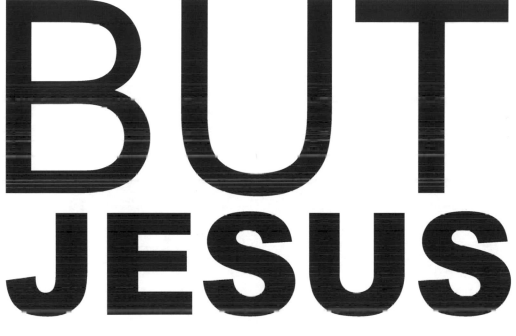

BUT JESUS

LOOKED AT THEM AND SAID...

"with man this is impossible, but with God all things are possible"

Matthew 19:26

FAITH AND FORGIVENESS

Today: Mood:

Today I Am Grateful For: Today's Scripture I Will Meditate On:

Today's Prayer: What This Scripture Means To Me:

Today I Pray For (Name The Person Who   I Forgive These People:
You Pray For And What The Prayer Is
Towards):

Today I Believe God Is Asking Me: Today I Will Let Go Of:

Today I Am Open To: Today I Free Myself From:

Today I Forgive Myself For: I Know That The Blood Of Christ:

By The Grace Of God I Am: I Have Faith That:

FAITH AND FORGIVENESS

Today: Mood:

Today I Am Grateful For: Today's Scripture I Will Meditate On:

Today's Prayer: What This Scripture Means To Me:

Today I Pray For (Name The Person Who   I Forgive These People.
You Pray For And What The Prayer Is
Towards):

Today I Believe God Is Asking Me: Today I Will Let Go Of:

Today I Am Open To: Today I Free Myself From:

Today I Forgive Myself For: I Know That The Blood Of Christ:

By The Grace Of God I Am: I Have Faith That:

In the same way, faith by itself, if it is not accompanied by action, is dead. James 2:17

FAITH AND FORGIVENESS

Today: Mood:

Today I Am Grateful For: Today's Scripture I Will Meditate On:

Today's Prayer: What This Scripture Means To Me:

Today I Pray For (Name The Person Who   I Forgive These People:
You Pray For And What The Prayer Is
Towards):

Today I Believe God Is Asking Me: Today I Will Let Go Of:

Today I Am Open To: Today I Free Myself From:

Today I Forgive Myself For: I Know That The Blood Of Christ:

By The Grace Of God I Am: I Have Faith That:

A LOVE LETTER TO MY YOUNGER SELF

FAITH AND FORGIVENESS

Today: Mood:

Today I Am Grateful For: Today's Scripture I Will Meditate On:

Today's Prayer: What This Scripture Means To Me:

Today I Pray For (Name The Person Who   I Forgive These People:
You Pray For And What The Prayer Is
Towards):

Today I Believe God Is Asking Me: Today I Will Let Go Of:

Today I Am Open To: Today I Free Myself From:

Today I Forgive Myself For: I Know That The Blood Of Christ:

By The Grace Of God I Am: I Have Faith That:

FAITH AND FORGIVENESS

Today: Mood:

Today I Am Grateful For: Today's Scripture I Will Meditate On:

Today's Prayer: What This Scripture Means To Me:

Today I Pray For (Name The Person Who   I Forgive These People.
You Pray For And What The Prayer Is
Towards):

Today I Believe God Is Asking Me: Today I Will Let Go Of:

Today I Am Open To: Today I Free Myself From:

Today I Forgive Myself For: I Know That The Blood Of Christ:

By The Grace Of God I Am: I Have Faith That:

FAITH AND FORGIVENESS

Today:

Mood:

Today I Am Grateful For:

Today's Scripture I Will Meditate On:

Today's Prayer:

What This Scripture Means To Me:

Today I Pray For (Name The Person Who You Pray For And What The Prayer Is Towards):

I Forgive These People:

Today I Believe God Is Asking Me:

Today I Will Let Go Of:

Today I Am Open To:

Today I Free Myself From:

Today I Forgive Myself For:

I Know That The Blood Of Christ:

By The Grace Of God I Am:

I Have Faith That:

FAITH AND FORGIVENESS

Today:

Mood:

Today I Am Grateful For:

Today's Scripture I Will Meditate On:

Today's Prayer:

What This Scripture Means To Me:

Today I Pray For (Name The Person Who You Pray For And What The Prayer Is Towards):

I Forgive These People:

Today I Believe God Is Asking Me:

Today I Will Let Go Of:

Today I Am Open To:

Today I Free Myself From:

Today I Forgive Myself For:

I Know That The Blood Of Christ:

By The Grace Of God I Am:

I Have Faith That:

A LOVE LETTER TO
MY PRESENT SELF

IF YOU FEED YOUR FAITH DAILY,

Your Fears Will Starve To Death.

FAITH AND FORGIVENESS

Today: Mood:

Today I Am Grateful For: Today's Scripture I Will Meditate On:

Today's Prayer: What This Scripture Means To Me:

Today I Pray For (Name The Person Who   I Forgive These People:
You Pray For And What The Prayer Is
Towards):

Today I Believe God Is Asking Me: Today I Will Let Go Of:

Today I Am Open To: Today I Free Myself From:

Today I Forgive Myself For: I Know That The Blood Of Christ:

By The Grace Of God I Am: I Have Faith That:

A LOVE LETTER TO
MY FUTURE SELF

FAITH AND FORGIVENESS

Today: Mood:

Today I Am Grateful For: Today's Scripture I Will Meditate On:

Today's Prayer: What This Scripture Means To Me:

Today I Pray For (Name The Person Who   I Forgive These People:
You Pray For And What The Prayer Is
Towards):

Today I Believe God Is Asking Me: Today I Will Let Go Of:

Today I Am Open To: Today I Free Myself From:

Today I Forgive Myself For: I Know That The Blood Of Christ:

By The Grace Of God I Am: I Have Faith That:

SPIRITUAL ACTION:

IN FAITH, SPEND SOME MONEY
TOWARDS WHAT YOU ARE BELIEVING
AND ASKING FOR IN PRAYER.

SECTION TWO
STRENGTH AND RENEWAL

STRENGTH

Today: Mood:

Today's Prayer: The Bible Scripture I Will Meditate On
                                          Today:

Today I Will Focus On: What This Bible Scripture Means To Me:

LATER IN THE DAY

What God Revealed To Me Today: Today God Used Me To:

I Stepped Out On Faith And: I Speak Over:

Today I Gave   Today I Served In This Way:

And It Made Me Feel

I thank Christ Jesus our Lord, who has given me strength, that he considered me faithful, appointing me to his service. I Timothy 1:12

STRENGTH

Today: Mood:

Today's Prayer: The Bible Scripture I Will Meditate On
                                          Today:

Today I Will Focus On: What This Bible Scripture Means To Me:

LATER IN THE DAY

What God Revealed To Me Today: Today God Used Me To:

I Stepped Out On Faith And: I Speak Over:

Today I Gave   Today I Served In This Way:

And It Made Me Feel

THEN

YOU WILL CALL ON ME

and come and pray to me, and
I will listen to you.
Jeremiah 29:12

STRENGTH

Today: Mood:

Today's Prayer: The Bible Scripture I Will Meditate On
                                          Today:

Today I Will Focus On: What This Bible Scripture Means To Me:

LATER IN THE DAY

What God Revealed To Me Today: Today God Used Me To:

I Stepped Out On Faith And: I Speak Over:

Today I Gave   Today I Served In This Way:

And It Made Me Feel

STRENGTH

Today: Mood:

Today's Prayer: The Bible Scripture I Will Meditate On
                                          Today:

Today I Will Focus On: What This Bible Scripture Means To Me:

LATER IN THE DAY

What God Revealed To Me Today: Today God Used Me To:

I Stepped Out On Faith And: I Speak Over:

Today I Gave   Today I Served In This Way:

And It Made Me Feel

The Lord does not look at the things man looks at. Man looks at the outward appearance, but the Lord looks at the heart. 1 Samuel 16:7

STRENGTH

Today:

Mood:

Today's Prayer:

The Bible Scripture I Will Meditate On Today:

Today I Will Focus On:

What This Bible Scripture Means To Me:

LATER IN THE DAY

What God Revealed To Me Today:

Today God Used Me To:

I Stepped Out On Faith And:

I Speak Over:

Today I Gave

Today I Served In This Way:

And It Made Me Feel

STRENGTH

Today: Mood:

Today's Prayer: The Bible Scripture I Will Meditate On
                                                Today:

Today I Will Focus On: What This Bible Scripture Means To Me:

LATER IN THE DAY

What God Revealed To Me Today: Today God Used Me To:

I Stepped Out On Faith And: I Speak Over:

Today I Gave   Today I Served In This Way:

And It Made Me Feel

EMBRACE
THE NEW YOU.

If They Took Back The Pain They
Caused, You Would Lose The
Strength You Gained.

THE
THING ABOUT
HITTING ROCK

Bottom Is That You Have More
Knowledge, Strength And A
Different Blueprint On Getting
Back Up. Wipe The Tears Away,
Dust The Dirt Off And Get Up.

STRENGTH

Today: Mood:

Today's Prayer: The Bible Scripture I Will Meditate On
                                          Today:

Today I Will Focus On: What This Bible Scripture Means To Me:

LATER IN THE DAY

What God Revealed To Me Today: Today God Used Me To:

I Stepped Out On Faith And: I Speak Over:

Today I Gave   Today I Served In This Way:

And It Made Me Feel

STRENGTH

Today: Mood:

Today's Prayer: The Bible Scripture I Will Meditate On
                                         Today:

Today I Will Focus On: What This Bible Scripture Means To Me:

LATER IN THE DAY

What God Revealed To Me Today: Today God Used Me To:

I Stepped Out On Faith And: I Speak Over:

Today I Gave   Today I Served In This Way:

And It Made Me Feel

STRENGTH

Today: Mood:

Today's Prayer: The Bible Scripture I Will Meditate On
                                            Today:

Today I Will Focus On: What This Bible Scripture Means To Me:

LATER IN THE DAY

What God Revealed To Me Today: Today God Used Me To:

I Stepped Out On Faith And: I Speak Over:

Today I Gave   Today I Served In This Way:

And It Made Me Feel

STRENGTH

Today: Mood:

Today's Prayer: The Bible Scripture I Will Meditate On
                                        Today:

Today I Will Focus On: What This Bible Scripture Means To Me:

LATER IN THE DAY

What God Revealed To Me Today: Today God Used Me To:

I Stepped Out On Faith And: I Speak Over:

Today I Gave   Today I Served In This Way:

And It Made Me Feel

IT'S TIME TO BUILD BACK THE
STRENGTH

To Be Who You Are!

Unapologetically.

THEY WON'T FULLY UNDERSTAND YOUR **STRENGTH,**

Because They Refuse To Acknowledge Your Struggle.
But Look At You. You Made It.

WILL CONTINUE TO EVOLVE.

I Am Not Put Here For One Purpose,
But For Many. God Grows Me And
For That Reason, Even When I Fall,
I Am Still Backed Up With Strength
And Divine Power.

STRENGTH

Today: Mood:

Today's Prayer: The Bible Scripture I Will Meditate On Today:

Today I Will Focus On: What This Bible Scripture Means To Me:

LATER IN THE DAY

What God Revealed To Me Today: Today God Used Me To:

I Stepped Out On Faith And: I Speak Over:

Today I Gave   Today I Served In This Way:

And It Made Me Feel

STRENGTH

Today: Mood:

Today's Prayer: The Bible Scripture I Will Meditate On
                                                Today:

Today I Will Focus On: What This Bible Scripture Means To Me:

LATER IN THE DAY

What God Revealed To Me Today: Today God Used Me To:

I Stepped Out On Faith And: I Speak Over:

Today I Gave   Today I Served In This Way:

And It Made Me Feel

STRENGTH

Today: Mood:

Today's Prayer: The Bible Scripture I Will Meditate On
                                          Today:

Today I Will Focus On: What This Bible Scripture Means To Me:

LATER IN THE DAY

What God Revealed To Me Today: Today God Used Me To:

I Stepped Out On Faith And: I Speak Over:

Today I Gave   Today I Served In This Way:

And It Made Me Feel

STRENGTH

Today: Mood:

Today's Prayer: The Bible Scripture I Will Meditate On
                                                Today:

Today I Will Focus On: What This Bible Scripture Means To Me:

LATER IN THE DAY

What God Revealed To Me Today: Today God Used Me To:

I Stepped Out On Faith And: I Speak Over:

Today I Gave   Today I Served In This Way:

And It Made Me Feel

I HAVE THE STRENGTH TO

STRENGTH

Today: Mood:

Today's Prayer: The Bible Scripture I Will Meditate On
                                            Today:

Today I Will Focus On: What This Bible Scripture Means To Me:

LATER IN THE DAY

What God Revealed To Me Today: Today God Used Me To:

I Stepped Out On Faith And: I Speak Over:

Today I Gave   Today I Served In This Way:

And It Made Me Feel

STRENGTH

Today: Mood:

Today's Prayer: The Bible Scripture I Will Meditate On
                                        Today:

Today I Will Focus On: What This Bible Scripture Means To Me:

LATER IN THE DAY

What God Revealed To Me Today: Today God Used Me To:

I Stepped Out On Faith And: I Speak Over:

Today I Gave   Today I Served In This Way:

And It Made Me Feel

But the Lord is faithful, and he will strengthen and protect you from the evil one. 2 Thessalonians 3:3

STRENGTH

Today: Mood:

Today's Prayer: The Bible Scripture I Will Meditate On
                                                Today:

Today I Will Focus On: What This Bible Scripture Means To Me:

LATER IN THE DAY

What God Revealed To Me Today: Today God Used Me To:

I Stepped Out On Faith And: I Speak Over:

Today I Gave   Today I Served In This Way:

And It Made Me Feel

STRENGTH

Today: Mood:

Today's Prayer: The Bible Scripture I Will Meditate On
                                          Today:

Today I Will Focus On: What This Bible Scripture Means To Me:

LATER IN THE DAY

What God Revealed To Me Today: Today God Used Me To:

I Stepped Out On Faith And: I Speak Over:

Today I Gave   Today I Served In This Way:

And It Made Me Feel

For the Spirit God gave us does not make us timid, but gives us power, love and self-discipline. 2 Timothy 1:7

THIS WEEK'S SPIRITUAL MOMENT THAT BROUGHT ABOUT CHANGE

STRENGTH

Today: Mood:

Today's Prayer: The Bible Scripture I Will Meditate On
                                                Today:

Today I Will Focus On: What This Bible Scripture Means To Me:

LATER IN THE DAY

What God Revealed To Me Today: Today God Used Me To:

I Stepped Out On Faith And: I Speak Over:

Today I Gave   Today I Served In This Way:

And It Made Me Feel

SPIRITUAL ACTION:

BE STILL TODAY. GET INTIMATE TODAY. TURN OFF ALL MEDIA SUCH AS TV, INTERNET AND MUSIC. THE WORK IS SPIRITUAL. DO LESS EXTERNALLY TO GET MORE INTERNALLY & EXTERNALLY.

STRENGTH

Today: Mood:

Today's Prayer: The Bible Scripture I Will Meditate On
                                          Today:

Today I Will Focus On: What This Bible Scripture Means To Me:

LATER IN THE DAY

What God Revealed To Me Today: Today God Used Me To:

I Stepped Out On Faith And: I Speak Over:

Today I Gave   Today I Served In This Way:

And It Made Me Feel

Bless those who persecute you; bless and do not curse. Romans 12:14

STRENGTH

Today: Mood:

Today's Prayer: The Bible Scripture I Will Meditate On
                                         Today:

Today I Will Focus On: What This Bible Scripture Means To Me:

LATER IN THE DAY

What God Revealed To Me Today: Today God Used Me To:

I Stepped Out On Faith And: I Speak Over:

Today I Gave   Today I Served In This Way:

And It Made Me Feel

STRENGTH

Today: Mood:

Today's Prayer: The Bible Scripture I Will Meditate On Today:

Today I Will Focus On: What This Bible Scripture Means To Me:

LATER IN THE DAY

What God Revealed To Me Today: Today God Used Me To:

I Stepped Out On Faith And: I Speak Over:

Today I Gave   Today I Served In This Way:

And It Made Me Feel

STRENGTH

Today: Mood:

Today's Prayer: The Bible Scripture I Will Meditate On
                                          Today:

Today I Will Focus On: What This Bible Scripture Means To Me:

LATER IN THE DAY

What God Revealed To Me Today: Today God Used Me To:

I Stepped Out On Faith And: I Speak Over:

Today I Gave   Today I Served In This Way:

And It Made Me Feel

TODAY'S LOVE
LETTER TO GOD

STRENGTH

Today: Mood:

Today's Prayer: The Bible Scripture I Will Meditate On
                                          Today:

Today I Will Focus On: What This Bible Scripture Means To Me:

LATER IN THE DAY

What God Revealed To Me Today: Today God Used Me To:

I Stepped Out On Faith And: I Speak Over:

Today I Gave   Today I Served In This Way:

And It Made Me Feel

STRENGTH

Today: Mood:

Today's Prayer: The Bible Scripture I Will Meditate On
                                                Today:

Today I Will Focus On: What This Bible Scripture Means To Me:

LATER IN THE DAY

What God Revealed To Me Today: Today God Used Me To:

I Stepped Out On Faith And: I Speak Over:

Today I Gave   Today I Served In This Way:

And It Made Me Feel

STRENGTH

Today: Mood:

Today's Prayer: The Bible Scripture I Will Meditate On
                                          Today:

Today I Will Focus On: What This Bible Scripture Means To Me:

LATER IN THE DAY

What God Revealed To Me Today: Today God Used Me To:

I Stepped Out On Faith And: I Speak Over:

Today I Gave   Today I Served In This Way:

And It Made Me Feel

HE
SAID YOU
HAVE THE
POWER

To Move Mountains
With Your Faith.

STRENGTH

Today: Mood:

Today's Prayer: The Bible Scripture I Will Meditate On
                                          Today:

Today I Will Focus On: What This Bible Scripture Means To Me:

LATER IN THE DAY

What God Revealed To Me Today: Today God Used Me To:

I Stepped Out On Faith And: I Speak Over:

Today I Gave   Today I Served In This Way:

And It Made Me Feel

STRENGTH

Today: Mood:

Today's Prayer: The Bible Scripture I Will Meditate On
                                      Today:

Today I Will Focus On: What This Bible Scripture Means To Me:

LATER IN THE DAY

What God Revealed To Me Today: Today God Used Me To:

I Stepped Out On Faith And: I Speak Over:

Today I Gave   Today I Served In This Way:

And It Made Me Feel

Be strong and courageous. Do not fear or be n dread of them, for it is the Lord your God who goes with you. He will not leave you or forsake you. Deuteronomy 31:6

IT'S OKAY IF THEY UNDERESTIMATE

YOU.
GOD
KNOWS.

Let His Power Show Within You.

No Need To Fight Back.

STRENGTH

Today: Mood:

Today's Prayer: The Bible Scripture I Will Meditate On
                                          Today:

Today I Will Focus On: What This Bible Scripture Means To Me:

LATER IN THE DAY

What God Revealed To Me Today: Today God Used Me To:

I Stepped Out On Faith And: I Speak Over:

Today I Gave   Today I Served In This Way:

And It Made Me Feel

STRENGTH

Today: Mood:

Today's Prayer: The Bible Scripture I Will Meditate On
                                                    Today:

Today I Will Focus On: What This Bible Scripture Means To Me:

LATER IN THE DAY

What God Revealed To Me Today: Today God Used Me To:

I Stepped Out On Faith And: I Speak Over:

Today I Gave   Today I Served In This Way:

And It Made Me Feel

STRENGTH

Today: Mood:

Today's Prayer: The Bible Scripture I Will Meditate On
                                                Today:

Today I Will Focus On: What This Bible Scripture Means To Me:

LATER IN THE DAY

What God Revealed To Me Today: Today God Used Me To:

I Stepped Out On Faith And: I Speak Over:

Today I Gave   Today I Served In This Way:

And It Made Me Feel

STRENGTH

Today:

Mood:

Today's Prayer:

The Bible Scripture I Will Meditate On Today:

Today I Will Focus On:

What This Bible Scripture Means To Me:

LATER IN THE DAY

What God Revealed To Me Today:

Today God Used Me To:

I Stepped Out On Faith And:

I Speak Over:

Today I Gave

Today I Served In This Way:

And It Made Me Feel

YOU

DON'T UNDERSTAND WHY
YOU WERE CHOSEN TO GO
THROUGH THE

STORM,

Because You Don't Understand
The Power Of Your Blessings
That Follow.

HAPPINESS
IS A POSITION OF
POWER.

STRENGTH

Today: Mood:

Today's Prayer: The Bible Scripture I Will Meditate On
                                    Today:

Today I Will Focus On: What This Bible Scripture Means To Me:

LATER IN THE DAY

What God Revealed To Me Today: Today God Used Me To:

I Stepped Out On Faith And: I Speak Over:

Today I Gave   Today I Served In This Way:

And It Made Me Feel

STRENGTH

Today: Mood:

Today's Prayer: The Bible Scripture I Will Meditate On
                                              Today:

Today I Will Focus On: What This Bible Scripture Means To Me:

LATER IN THE DAY

What God Revealed To Me Today: Today God Used Me To:

I Stepped Out On Faith And: I Speak Over:

Today I Gave   Today I Served In This Way:

And It Made Me Feel

LOVE.

I CAME FROM IT.

I'M ALIVE BECAUSE OF IT.

IT'S MY BIRTHRIGHT TO HAVE IT.

SO I WILL ALWAYS OPERATE IN IT.

BECAUSE I FLOURISH IN IT.

GOD IS LOVE.

STRENGTH

Today: Mood:

Today's Prayer: The Bible Scripture I Will Meditate On
                                          Today:

Today I Will Focus On: What This Bible Scripture Means To Me:

LATER IN THE DAY

What God Revealed To Me Today: Today God Used Me To:

I Stepped Out On Faith And: I Speak Over:

Today I Gave   Today I Served In This Way:

And It Made Me Feel

STRENGTH

Today: Mood:

Today's Prayer: The Bible Scripture I Will Meditate On
                                          Today:

Today I Will Focus On: What This Bible Scripture Means To Me:

LATER IN THE DAY

What God Revealed To Me Today: Today God Used Me To:

I Stepped Out On Faith And: I Speak Over:

Today I Gave   Today I Served In This Way:

And It Made Me Feel

STRENGTH

Today: Mood:

Today's Prayer: The Bible Scripture I Will Meditate On
                                                Today:

Today I Will Focus On: What This Bible Scripture Means To Me:

LATER IN THE DAY

What God Revealed To Me Today: Today God Used Me To:

I Stepped Out On Faith And: I Speak Over:

Today I Gave   Today I Served In This Way:

And It Made Me Feel

STRENGTH

Today: Mood:

Today's Prayer: The Bible Scripture I Will Meditate On
                                         Today:

Today I Will Focus On: What This Bible Scripture Means To Me:

LATER IN THE DAY

What God Revealed To Me Today: Today God Used Me To:

I Stepped Out On Faith And: I Speak Over:

Today I Gave   Today I Served In This Way:

And It Made Me Feel

STRENGTH

Today: Mood:

Today's Prayer: The Bible Scripture I Will Meditate On
                                          Today:

Today I Will Focus On: What This Bible Scripture Means To Me:

LATER IN THE DAY

What God Revealed To Me Today: Today God Used Me To:

I Stepped Out On Faith And: I Speak Over:

Today I Gave   Today I Served In This Way:

And It Made Me Feel

LATELY GOD HAS BEEN SHOWING ME

STRENGTH

Today: Mood:

Today's Prayer: The Bible Scripture I Will Meditate On
                                Today:

Today I Will Focus On: What This Bible Scripture Means To Me:

LATER IN THE DAY

What God Revealed To Me Today: Today God Used Me To:

I Stepped Out On Faith And: I Speak Over:

Today I Gave   Today I Served In This Way:

And It Made Me Feel

STRENGTH

Today: Mood:

Today's Prayer: The Bible Scripture I Will Meditate On
                                          Today:

Today I Will Focus On: What This Bible Scripture Means To Me:

LATER IN THE DAY

What God Revealed To Me Today: Today God Used Me To:

I Stepped Out On Faith And: I Speak Over:

Today I Gave   Today I Served In This Way:

And It Made Me Feel

STRENGTH

Today: Mood:

Today's Prayer: The Bible Scripture I Will Meditate On
                                          Today:

Today I Will Focus On: What This Bible Scripture Means To Me:

LATER IN THE DAY

What God Revealed To Me Today: Today God Used Me To:

I Stepped Out On Faith And: I Speak Over:

Today I Gave   Today I Served In This Way:

And It Made Me Feel

STRENGTH

Today: Mood:

Today's Prayer: The Bible Scripture I Will Meditate On
                                         Today:

Today I Will Focus On: What This Bible Scripture Means To Me:

LATER IN THE DAY

What God Revealed To Me Today: Today God Used Me To:

I Stepped Out On Faith And: I Speak Over:

Today I Gave   Today I Served In This Way:

And It Made Me Feel

SPIRITUAL ACTION:

TIME TO DETOX. THIS IS A SPIRITUAL
DIET. EVALUATE WHAT IT IS
YOU CONSUME THROUGH MEDIA,
CONVERSATIONS YOU PARTICIPATE IN
AND WHAT YOU EAT. DECIDE TODAY
WHAT WILL NO LONGER COME
IN-BETWEEN YOUR TIME WITH
YOU AND GOD.

STRENGTH

Today: Mood:

Today's Prayer: The Bible Scripture I Will Meditate On
                                          Today:

Today I Will Focus On: What This Bible Scripture Means To Me:

LATER IN THE DAY

What God Revealed To Me Today: Today God Used Me To:

I Stepped Out On Faith And: I Speak Over:

Today I Gave   Today I Served In This Way:

And It Made Me Feel

STRENGTH

Today:

Mood:

Today's Prayer:

The Bible Scripture I Will Meditate On Today:

Today I Will Focus On:

What This Bible Scripture Means To Me:

LATER IN THE DAY

What God Revealed To Me Today:

Today God Used Me To:

I Stepped Out On Faith And:

I Speak Over:

Today I Gave

Today I Served In This Way:

And It Made Me Feel

DON'T FORCE WHAT
GOD
Can Do Naturally.

NOT
GETTING

What You Want Now Is Just
Setting You Up To Getting
What You Need Real Soon.

STRENGTH

Today: Mood:

Today's Prayer: The Bible Scripture I Will Meditate On
                                          Today:

Today I Will Focus On: What This Bible Scripture Means To Me:

LATER IN THE DAY

What God Revealed To Me Today: Today God Used Me To:

I Stepped Out On Faith And: I Speak Over:

Today I Gave   Today I Served In This Way:

And It Made Me Feel

Whoever gives heed to instruction prospers, and blessed is the one who trusts in the Lord. Proverbs 16:20

STRENGTH

Today: Mood:

Today's Prayer: The Bible Scripture I Will Meditate On
                                                Today:

Today I Will Focus On: What This Bible Scripture Means To Me:

LATER IN THE DAY

What God Revealed To Me Today: Today God Used Me To:

I Stepped Out On Faith And: I Speak Over:

Today I Gave   Today I Served In This Way:

And It Made Me Feel

I WANT TO GROW IN

STRENGTH

Today: Mood:

Today's Prayer: The Bible Scripture I Will Meditate On
                                          Today:

Today I Will Focus On: What This Bible Scripture Means To Me:

LATER IN THE DAY

What God Revealed To Me Today: Today God Used Me To:

I Stepped Out On Faith And: I Speak Over:

Today I Gave   Today I Served In This Way:

And It Made Me Feel

STRENGTH

Today: Mood:

Today's Prayer: The Bible Scripture I Will Meditate On
                                          Today:

Today I Will Focus On: What This Bible Scripture Means To Me:

LATER IN THE DAY

What God Revealed To Me Today: Today God Used Me To:

I Stepped Out On Faith And: I Speak Over:

Today I Gave   Today I Served In This Way:

And It Made Me Feel

STRENGTH

Today: Mood:

Today's Prayer: The Bible Scripture I Will Meditate On
                                          Today:

Today I Will Focus On: What This Bible Scripture Means To Me:

LATER IN THE DAY

What God Revealed To Me Today: Today God Used Me To:

I Stepped Out On Faith And: I Speak Over:

Today I Gave   Today I Served In This Way:

And It Made Me Feel

172

TRUST IN THE
LORD

with all your heart, and lean not on your own understanding; in all your ways acknowledge Him, and He shall direct your paths. Proverbs 3:5-6

STRENGTH

Today: Mood:

Today's Prayer: The Bible Scripture I Will Meditate On
                                          Today:

Today I Will Focus On: What This Bible Scripture Means To Me:

LATER IN THE DAY

What God Revealed To Me Today: Today God Used Me To:

I Stepped Out On Faith And: I Speak Over:

Today I Gave   Today I Served In This Way:

And It Made Me Feel

STRENGTH

Today: Mood:

Today's Prayer: The Bible Scripture I Will Meditate On
                                          Today:

Today I Will Focus On: What This Bible Scripture Means To Me:

LATER IN THE DAY

What God Revealed To Me Today: Today God Used Me To:

I Stepped Out On Faith And: I Speak Over:

Today I Gave   Today I Served In This Way:

And It Made Me Feel

STRENGTH

Today: Mood:

Today's Prayer: The Bible Scripture I Will Meditate On
                                                 Today:

Today I Will Focus On: What This Bible Scripture Means To Me:

LATER IN THE DAY

What God Revealed To Me Today: Today God Used Me To:

I Stepped Out On Faith And: I Speak Over:

Today I Gave   Today I Served In This Way:

And It Made Me Feel

SPIRITUAL NOTES

STRENGTH

Today: Mood:

Today's Prayer: The Bible Scripture I Will Meditate On
                                                Today:

Today I Will Focus On: What This Bible Scripture Means To Me:

LATER IN THE DAY

What God Revealed To Me Today: Today God Used Me To:

I Stepped Out On Faith And: I Speak Over:

Today I Gave   Today I Served In This Way:

And It Made Me Feel

STRENGTH

Today: Mood:

Today's Prayer: The Bible Scripture I Will Meditate On
                                            Today:

Today I Will Focus On: What This Bible Scripture Means To Me:

LATER IN THE DAY

What God Revealed To Me Today: Today God Used Me To:

I Stepped Out On Faith And: I Speak Over:

Today I Gave   Today I Served In This Way:

And It Made Me Feel

But I will hope continually and will praise you yet more and more. Psalm 71:14

I AM WORKING TOWARDS

STRENGTH

Today:

Mood:

Today's Prayer:

The Bible Scripture I Will Meditate On Today:

Today I Will Focus On:

What This Bible Scripture Means To Me:

LATER IN THE DAY

What God Revealed To Me Today:

Today God Used Me To:

I Stepped Out On Faith And:

I Speak Over:

Today I Gave

Today I Served In This Way:

And It Made Me Feel

STRENGTH

Today:

Mood:

Today's Prayer:

The Bible Scripture I Will Meditate On Today:

Today I Will Focus On:

What This Bible Scripture Means To Me:

LATER IN THE DAY

What God Revealed To Me Today:

Today God Used Me To:

I Stepped Out On Faith And:

I Speak Over:

Today I Gave

Today I Served In This Way:

And It Made Me Feel

182

YOUR
STRUGGLE
Will Transform Into Your Testimony

STRENGTH

Today: Mood:

Today's Prayer: The Bible Scripture I Will Meditate On
                                          Today:

Today I Will Focus On: What This Bible Scripture Means To Me:

LATER IN THE DAY

What God Revealed To Me Today: Today God Used Me To:

I Stepped Out On Faith And: I Speak Over:

Today I Gave   Today I Served In This Way:

And It Made Me Feel

STRENGTH

Today:

Today's Prayer:

Today I Will Focus On:

Mood:

The Bible Scripture I Will Meditate On Today:

What This Bible Scripture Means To Me:

LATER IN THE DAY

What God Revealed To Me Today:

I Stepped Out On Faith And:

Today I Gave

And It Made Me Feel

Today God Used Me To:

I Speak Over:

Today I Served In This Way:

STRENGTH

Today:

Mood:

Today's Prayer:

The Bible Scripture I Will Meditate On Today:

Today I Will Focus On:

What This Bible Scripture Means To Me:

LATER IN THE DAY

What God Revealed To Me Today:

Today God Used Me To:

I Stepped Out On Faith And:

I Speak Over:

Today I Gave

Today I Served In This Way:

And It Made Me Feel

SECTION THREE

THE WORK.
THE TRUTH IN
BREAKTHROUGHS AND
MIRACLES

BREAKTHROUGHS AND MIRACLES

Today: Mood:

Today I Am Grateful For: Today's Prayer:

Today I Believe: Today I Am Making My Life Simple And
                                          Light By:

Today's Daydream: I Am Obeying The Spirit Within Me And
                                          Will Take Action On:

I Know I Am Not Limited To: Today I Will Invest In Myself By:

Today I Will Invest In Others By: My Previous Breakthrough Taught Me:

The Breakthrough I Received Today: The Miracle That Happened Today:

BREAKTHROUGHS AND MIRACLES

Today: Mood:

Today I Am Grateful For: Today's Prayer:

Today I Believe: Today I Am Making My Life Simple And
                                                Light By:

Today's Daydream: I Am Obeying The Spirit Within Me And
                                                Will Take Action On:

I Know I Am Not Limited To: Today I Will Invest In Myself By:

Today I Will Invest In Others By: My Previous Breakthrough Taught Me:

The Breakthrough I Received Today: The Miracle That Happened Today:

BREAKTHROUGHS AND MIRACLES

Today:

Mood:

Today I Am Grateful For:

Today's Prayer:

Today I Believe:

Today I Am Making My Life Simple And Light By:

Today's Daydream:

I Am Obeying The Spirit Within Me And Will Take Action On:

I Know I Am Not Limited To:

Today I Will Invest In Myself By:

Today I Will Invest In Others By:

My Previous Breakthrough Taught Me:

The Breakthrough I Received Today:

The Miracle That Happened Today:

BREAKTHROUGHS AND MIRACLES

Today:

Today I Am Grateful For:

Mood:

Today's Prayer:

Today I Believe:

Today I Am Making My Life Simple And Light By:

Today's Daydream:

I Am Obeying The Spirit Within Me And Will Take Action On:

I Know I Am Not Limited To:

Today I Will Invest In Myself By:

Today I Will Invest In Others By:

My Previous Breakthrough Taught Me:

The Breakthrough I Received Today:

The Miracle That Happened Today:

For in this hope we were saved. Now hope that is seen is not hope. For who hopes for what he sees? Romans 8:24

AS SOON AS YOU LET GO OF YOUR **WORRIES,** Watch The Miracles Pour In.

BREAKTHROUGHS AND MIRACLES

Today:

Mood:

Today I Am Grateful For:

Today's Prayer:

Today I Believe:

Today I Am Making My Life Simple And Light By:

Today's Daydream:

I Am Obeying The Spirit Within Me And Will Take Action On:

I Know I Am Not Limited To:

Today I Will Invest In Myself By:

Today I Will Invest In Others By:

My Previous Breakthrough Taught Me:

The Breakthrough I Received Today:

The Miracle That Happened Today:

Jesus looked at them and said, "With man this is impossible, but not with God; all things are possible with God." Mark 10:27

BREAKTHROUGHS AND MIRACLES

Today: Mood:

Today I Am Grateful For: Today's Prayer:

Today I Believe: Today I Am Making My Life Simple And
                                          Light By:

Today's Daydream: I Am Obeying The Spirit Within Me And
                                          Will Take Action On:

I Know I Am Not Limited To: Today I Will Invest In Myself By:

Today I Will Invest In Others By: My Previous Breakthrough Taught Me:

The Breakthrough I Received Today: The Miracle That Happened Today:

I AM A
MAGNET
For Miracles Because I Believe

BREAKTHROUGHS AND MIRACLES

Today: Mood:

Today I Am Grateful For: Today's Prayer:

Today I Believe: Today I Am Making My Life Simple And
                                      Light By:

Today's Daydream: I Am Obeying The Spirit Within Me And
                                      Will Take Action On:

I Know I Am Not Limited To: Today I Will Invest In Myself By:

Today I Will Invest In Others By: My Previous Breakthrough Taught Me:

The Breakthrough I Received Today: The Miracle That Happened Today:

For no word from God will ever fail. Luke 1:37

BREAKTHROUGHS AND MIRACLES

Today:

Today I Am Grateful For:

Today I Believe:

Today's Daydream:

I Know I Am Not Limited To:

Today I Will Invest In Others By:

The Breakthrough I Received Today:

Mood:

Today's Prayer:

Today I Am Making My Life Simple And Light By:

I Am Obeying The Spirit Within Me And Will Take Action On:

Today I Will Invest In Myself By:

My Previous Breakthrough Taught Me:

The Miracle That Happened Today:

I will give thanks to you, Lord, with all my heart; I will tell of all your wonderful deeds. Psalm 9:1

THE BIGGEST MIRACLE I AM EXPECTING

HE CAN STILL PERFORM
MIRACLES.

You Just Have To Believe.
The King Of Kings.

BREAKTHROUGHS AND MIRACLES

Today: Mood:

Today I Am Grateful For: Today's Prayer:

Today I Believe: Today I Am Making My Life Simple And
                                                Light By:

Today's Daydream: I Am Obeying The Spirit Within Me And
                                                Will Take Action On:

I Know I Am Not Limited To: Today I Will Invest In Myself By:

Today I Will Invest In Others By: My Previous Breakthrough Taught Me:

The Breakthrough I Received Today: The Miracle That Happened Today:

BREAKTHROUGHS AND MIRACLES

Today: Mood:

Today I Am Grateful For: Today's Prayer:

Today I Believe: Today I Am Making My Life Simple And
                                                Light By:

Today's Daydream: I Am Obeying The Spirit Within Me And
                                                Will Take Action On:

I Know I Am Not Limited To: Today I Will Invest In Myself By:

Today I Will Invest In Others By: My Previous Breakthrough Taught Me:

The Breakthrough I Received Today: The Miracle That Happened Today:

BREAKTHROUGHS AND MIRACLES

Today:

Mood:

Today I Am Grateful For:

Today's Prayer:

Today I Believe:

Today I Am Making My Life Simple And Light By:

Today's Daydream:

I Am Obeying The Spirit Within Me And Will Take Action On:

I Know I Am Not Limited To:

Today I Will Invest In Myself By:

Today I Will Invest In Others By:

My Previous Breakthrough Taught Me:

The Breakthrough I Received Today:

The Miracle That Happened Today:

SPIRITUAL ACTION:

GO FOR A FIFTEEN MINUTE
WALK AND SPEAK TO YOUR
BREAKTHROUGH OUT LOUD. REPEAT
THE BREAKTHROUGH YOU ARE
EXPECTING THROUGHOUT YOUR
WALK. SAY IT AND BELIEVE IT.

BREAKTHROUGHS AND MIRACLES

Today: Mood:

Today I Am Grateful For: Today's Prayer:

Today I Believe: Today I Am Making My Life Simple And
                                          Light By:

Today's Daydream: I Am Obeying The Spirit Within Me And
                                          Will Take Action On:

I Know I Am Not Limited To: Today I Will Invest In Myself By:

Today I Will Invest In Others By: My Previous Breakthrough Taught Me:

The Breakthrough I Received Today: The Miracle That Happened Today:

LIFT MY EYES TO THE HILLS—
WHERE DOES MY

HELP

COME FROM?
My Help Comes From The
Lord, The Maker Of Heaven
And Earth."
—Psalm 121:1–2

BREAKTHROUGHS AND MIRACLES

Today: Mood:

Today I Am Grateful For: Today's Prayer:

Today I Believe: Today I Am Making My Life Simple And
                                          Light By:

Today's Daydream: I Am Obeying The Spirit Within Me And
                                          Will Take Action On:

I Know I Am Not Limited To: Today I Will Invest In Myself By:

Today I Will Invest In Others By: My Previous Breakthrough Taught Me:

The Breakthrough I Received Today: The Miracle That Happened Today:

BREAKTHROUGHS AND MIRACLES

Today:

Mood:

Today I Am Grateful For:

Today's Prayer:

Today I Believe:

Today I Am Making My Life Simple And Light By:

Today's Daydream:

I Am Obeying The Spirit Within Me And Will Take Action On:

I Know I Am Not Limited To:

Today I Will Invest In Myself By:

Today I Will Invest In Others By:

My Previous Breakthrough Taught Me:

The Breakthrough I Received Today:

The Miracle That Happened Today:

YOU

AREN'T SUPPOSE TO KNOW WHEN THE

MIRACLE

WILL HAPPEN.

You're Just Suppose To Expect It.

BREAKTHROUGHS AND MIRACLES

Today:

Today I Am Grateful For:

Today I Believe:

Today's Daydream:

I Know I Am Not Limited To:

Today I Will Invest In Others By:

The Breakthrough I Received Today:

Mood:

Today's Prayer:

Today I Am Making My Life Simple And Light By:

I Am Obeying The Spirit Within Me And Will Take Action On:

Today I Will Invest In Myself By:

My Previous Breakthrough Taught Me:

The Miracle That Happened Today:

BREAKTHROUGHS AND MIRACLES

Today:

Mood:

Today I Am Grateful For:

Today's Prayer:

Today I Believe:

Today I Am Making My Life Simple And Light By:

Today's Daydream:

I Am Obeying The Spirit Within Me And Will Take Action On:

I Know I Am Not Limited To:

Today I Will Invest In Myself By:

Today I Will Invest In Others By:

My Previous Breakthrough Taught Me:

The Breakthrough I Received Today:

The Miracle That Happened Today:

BREAKTHROUGHS AND MIRACLES

Today:

Mood:

Today I Am Grateful For:

Today's Prayer:

Today I Believe:

Today I Am Making My Life Simple And Light By:

Today's Daydream:

I Am Obeying The Spirit Within Me And Will Take Action On:

I Know I Am Not Limited To:

Today I Will Invest In Myself By:

Today I Will Invest In Others By:

My Previous Breakthrough Taught Me:

The Breakthrough I Received Today:

The Miracle That Happened Today:

From my distress I called upon the LORD; The LORD answered me and set me in a large place. Psalm 118:5

BREAKTHROUGHS AND MIRACLES

Today:

Mood:

Today I Am Grateful For:

Today's Prayer:

Today I Believe:

Today I Am Making My Life Simple And Light By:

Today's Daydream:

I Am Obeying The Spirit Within Me And Will Take Action On:

I Know I Am Not Limited To:

Today I Will Invest In Myself By:

Today I Will Invest In Others By:

My Previous Breakthrough Taught Me:

The Breakthrough I Received Today:

The Miracle That Happened Today:

YOUR

WAIT WON'T MAKE SENSE.

But Neither Will Your Miracle. Just Expect It.

BREAKTHROUGHS AND MIRACLES

Today:

Mood:

Today I Am Grateful For:

Today's Prayer:

Today I Believe:

Today I Am Making My Life Simple And Light By:

Today's Daydream:

I Am Obeying The Spirit Within Me And Will Take Action On:

I Know I Am Not Limited To:

Today I Will Invest In Myself By:

Today I Will Invest In Others By:

My Previous Breakthrough Taught Me:

The Breakthrough I Received Today:

The Miracle That Happened Today:

BREAKTHROUGHS AND MIRACLES

Today:

Mood:

Today I Am Grateful For:

Today's Prayer:

Today I Believe:

Today I Am Making My Life Simple And Light By:

Today's Daydream:

I Am Obeying The Spirit Within Me And Will Take Action On:

I Know I Am Not Limited To:

Today I Will Invest In Myself By:

Today I Will Invest In Others By:

My Previous Breakthrough Taught Me:

The Breakthrough I Received Today:

The Miracle That Happened Today:

Give thanks to the God of heaven, for his steadfast love endures forever. Psalm 136:26

BREAKTHROUGHS AND MIRACLES

Today:

Mood:

Today I Am Grateful For:

Today's Prayer:

Today I Believe:

Today I Am Making My Life Simple And Light By:

Today's Daydream:

I Am Obeying The Spirit Within Me And Will Take Action On:

I Know I Am Not Limited To:

Today I Will Invest In Myself By:

Today I Will Invest In Others By:

My Previous Breakthrough Taught Me:

The Breakthrough I Received Today:

The Miracle That Happened Today:

The name of the LORD is a fortified tower; the righteous run to it and are safe. Proverbs 18:10

MY CURRENT BREAKTHROUGH

BREAKTHROUGHS AND MIRACLES

Today: Mood:

Today I Am Grateful For: Today's Prayer:

Today I Believe: Today I Am Making My Life Simple And
                                                Light By:

Today's Daydream: I Am Obeying The Spirit Within Me And
                                                Will Take Action On:

I Know I Am Not Limited To: Today I Will Invest In Myself By:

Today I Will Invest In Others By: My Previous Breakthrough Taught Me:

The Breakthrough I Received Today: The Miracle That Happened Today:

BREAKTHROUGHS AND MIRACLES

Today: Mood:

Today I Am Grateful For: Today's Prayer:

Today I Believe: Today I Am Making My Life Simple And
                                                Light By:

Today's Daydream: I Am Obeying The Spirit Within Me And
                                                Will Take Action On:

I Know I Am Not Limited To: Today I Will Invest In Myself By:

Today I Will Invest In Others By: My Previous Breakthrough Taught Me:

The Breakthrough I Received Today: The Miracle That Happened Today:

BREAKTHROUGHS AND MIRACLES

Today: Mood:

Today I Am Grateful For: Today's Prayer:

Today I Believe: Today I Am Making My Life Simple And
                                                Light By:

Today's Daydream: I Am Obeying The Spirit Within Me And
                                                Will Take Action On:

I Know I Am Not Limited To: Today I Will Invest In Myself By:

Today I Will Invest In Others By: My Previous Breakthrough Taught Me:

The Breakthrough I Received Today: The Miracle That Happened Today:

BREAKTHROUGHS AND MIRACLES

Today:

Today I Am Grateful For:

Today I Believe:

Today's Daydream:

I Know I Am Not Limited To:

Today I Will Invest In Others By:

The Breakthrough I Received Today:

Mood:

Today's Prayer:

Today I Am Making My Life Simple And Light By:

I Am Obeying The Spirit Within Me And Will Take Action On:

Today I Will Invest In Myself By:

My Previous Breakthrough Taught Me:

The Miracle That Happened Today:

LOVE NOTE TO GOD

REMEMBER THE SAME
GOD
Who Provided The Last Miracle Will Provide The Next.

BREAKTHROUGHS AND MIRACLES

Today: Mood:

Today I Am Grateful For: Today's Prayer:

Today I Believe: Today I Am Making My Life Simple And
                                          Light By:

Today's Daydream: I Am Obeying The Spirit Within Me And
                                          Will Take Action On:

I Know I Am Not Limited To: Today I Will Invest In Myself By:

Today I Will Invest In Others By: My Previous Breakthrough Taught Me:

The Breakthrough I Received Today: The Miracle That Happened Today:

BREAKTHROUGHS AND MIRACLES

Today:

Today I Am Grateful For:

Today I Believe:

Today's Daydream:

I Know I Am Not Limited To:

Today I Will Invest In Others By:

The Breakthrough I Received Today:

Mood:

Today's Prayer:

Today I Am Making My Life Simple And Light By:

I Am Obeying The Spirit Within Me And Will Take Action On:

Today I Will Invest In Myself By:

My Previous Breakthrough Taught Me:

The Miracle That Happened Today:

BREAKTHROUGHS AND MIRACLES

Today:

Mood:

Today I Am Grateful For:

Today's Prayer:

Today I Believe:

Today I Am Making My Life Simple And Light By:

Today's Daydream:

I Am Obeying The Spirit Within Me And Will Take Action On:

I Know I Am Not Limited To:

Today I Will Invest In Myself By:

Today I Will Invest In Others By:

My Previous Breakthrough Taught Me:

The Breakthrough I Received Today:

The Miracle That Happened Today:

BREAKTHROUGHS AND MIRACLES

Today:

Mood:

Today I Am Grateful For:

Today's Prayer:

Today I Believe:

Today I Am Making My Life Simple And Light By:

Today's Daydream:

I Am Obeying The Spirit Within Me And Will Take Action On:

I Know I Am Not Limited To:

Today I Will Invest In Myself By:

Today I Will Invest In Others By:

My Previous Breakthrough Taught Me:

The Breakthrough I Received Today:

The Miracle That Happened Today:

BREAKTHROUGHS AND MIRACLES

Today: Mood:

Today I Am Grateful For: Today's Prayer:

Today I Believe: Today I Am Making My Life Simple And
                                          Light By:

Today's Daydream: I Am Obeying The Spirit Within Me And
                                          Will Take Action On:

I Know I Am Not Limited To: Today I Will Invest In Myself By:

Today I Will Invest In Others By: My Previous Breakthrough Taught Me:

The Breakthrough I Received Today: The Miracle That Happened Today:

BREAKTHROUGHS AND MIRACLES

Today:

Today I Am Grateful For:

Today I Believe:

Today's Daydream:

I Know I Am Not Limited To:

Today I Will Invest In Others By:

The Breakthrough I Received Today:

Mood:

Today's Prayer:

Today I Am Making My Life Simple And Light By:

I Am Obeying The Spirit Within Me And Will Take Action On:

Today I Will Invest In Myself By:

My Previous Breakthrough Taught Me:

The Miracle That Happened Today:

ANOTHER STORM, ANOTHER MIRACLE.

WHEN YOUR BELIEFS ARE IN

HARMONY

With Your Words And Actions......

MIRACLES HAPPEN.

BREAKTHROUGHS AND MIRACLES

Today: Mood:

Today I Am Grateful For: Today's Prayer:

Today I Believe: Today I Am Making My Life Simple And
                                                Light By:

Today's Daydream: I Am Obeying The Spirit Within Me And
                                                Will Take Action On:

I Know I Am Not Limited To: Today I Will Invest In Myself By:

Today I Will Invest In Others By: My Previous Breakthrough Taught Me:

The Breakthrough I Received Today: The Miracle That Happened Today:

BREAKTHROUGHS AND MIRACLES

Today:

Mood:

Today I Am Grateful For:

Today's Prayer:

Today I Believe:

Today I Am Making My Life Simple And Light By:

Today's Daydream:

I Am Obeying The Spirit Within Me And Will Take Action On:

I Know I Am Not Limited To:

Today I Will Invest In Myself By:

Today I Will Invest In Others By:

My Previous Breakthrough Taught Me:

The Breakthrough I Received Today:

The Miracle That Happened Today:

BREAKTHROUGHS AND MIRACLES

Today: Mood:

Today I Am Grateful For: Today's Prayer:

Today I Believe: Today I Am Making My Life Simple And
                                                Light By:

Today's Daydream: I Am Obeying The Spirit Within Me And
                                                Will Take Action On:

I Know I Am Not Limited To: Today I Will Invest In Myself By:

Today I Will Invest In Others By: My Previous Breakthrough Taught Me:

The Breakthrough I Received Today: The Miracle That Happened Today:

BREAKTHROUGHS AND MIRACLES

Today:

Today I Am Grateful For:

Today I Believe:

Today's Daydream:

I Know I Am Not Limited To:

Today I Will Invest In Others By:

The Breakthrough I Received Today:

Mood:

Today's Prayer:

Today I Am Making My Life Simple And Light By:

I Am Obeying The Spirit Within Me And Will Take Action On:

Today I Will Invest In Myself By:

My Previous Breakthrough Taught Me:

The Miracle That Happened Today:

I AM SOMEONE'S

MIRACLE.

BREAKTHROUGHS AND MIRACLES

Today:

Today I Am Grateful For:

Today I Believe:

Today's Daydream:

I Know I Am Not Limited To:

Today I Will Invest In Others By:

The Breakthrough I Received Today:

Mood:

Today's Prayer:

Today I Am Making My Life Simple And Light By:

I Am Obeying The Spirit Within Me And Will Take Action On:

Today I Will Invest In Myself By:

My Previous Breakthrough Taught Me:

The Miracle That Happened Today:

We know that in everything God works for good with those who love him, who are called according to his purpose. Romans 8:28

BREAKTHROUGHS AND MIRACLES

Today: Mood:

Today I Am Grateful For: Today's Prayer:

Today I Believe: Today I Am Making My Life Simple And
                                                Light By:

Today's Daydream: I Am Obeying The Spirit Within Me And
                                                Will Take Action On:

I Know I Am Not Limited To: Today I Will Invest In Myself By:

Today I Will Invest In Others By: My Previous Breakthrough Taught Me:

The Breakthrough I Received Today: The Miracle That Happened Today:

BREAKTHROUGHS AND MIRACLES

Today:

Mood:

Today I Am Grateful For:

Today's Prayer:

Today I Believe:

Today I Am Making My Life Simple And Light By:

Today's Daydream:

I Am Obeying The Spirit Within Me And Will Take Action On:

I Know I Am Not Limited To:

Today I Will Invest In Myself By:

Today I Will Invest In Others By:

My Previous Breakthrough Taught Me:

The Breakthrough I Received Today:

The Miracle That Happened Today:

Come to me, all you who are weary and burdened, and I will give you rest. Matthew 11:28

BREAKTHROUGHS AND MIRACLES

Today: Mood:

Today I Am Grateful For: Today's Prayer:

Today I Believe: Today I Am Making My Life Simple And
                                                Light By:

Today's Daydream: I Am Obeying The Spirit Within Me And
                                                Will Take Action On:

I Know I Am Not Limited To: Today I Will Invest In Myself By:

Today I Will Invest In Others By: My Previous Breakthrough Taught Me:

The Breakthrough I Received Today: The Miracle That Happened Today:

BREAKTHROUGHS AND MIRACLES

Today:

Mood:

Today I Am Grateful For:

Today's Prayer:

Today I Believe:

Today I Am Making My Life Simple And Light By:

Today's Daydream:

I Am Obeying The Spirit Within Me And Will Take Action On:

I Know I Am Not Limited To:

Today I Will Invest In Myself By:

Today I Will Invest In Others By:

My Previous Breakthrough Taught Me:

The Breakthrough I Received Today:

The Miracle That Happened Today:

I WILL STEP OUT ON FAITH BY

BREAKTHROUGHS AND MIRACLES

Today:

Today I Am Grateful For:

Today I Believe:

Today's Daydream:

I Know I Am Not Limited To:

Today I Will Invest In Others By:

The Breakthrough I Received Today:

Mood:

Today's Prayer:

Today I Am Making My Life Simple And Light By:

I Am Obeying The Spirit Within Me And Will Take Action On:

Today I Will Invest In Myself By:

My Previous Breakthrough Taught Me:

The Miracle That Happened Today:

BREAKTHROUGHS AND MIRACLES

Today:

Mood:

Today I Am Grateful For:

Today's Prayer:

Today I Believe:

Today I Am Making My Life Simple And Light By:

Today's Daydream:

I Am Obeying The Spirit Within Me And Will Take Action On:

I Know I Am Not Limited To:

Today I Will Invest In Myself By:

Today I Will Invest In Others By:

My Previous Breakthrough Taught Me:

The Breakthrough I Received Today:

The Miracle That Happened Today:

BREAKTHROUGHS AND MIRACLES

Today: Mood:

Today I Am Grateful For: Today's Prayer:

Today I Believe: Today I Am Making My Life Simple And
                                          Light By:

Today's Daydream.   I Am Obeying The Spirit Within Me And
                                          Will Take Action On:

I Know I Am Not Limited To: Today I Will Invest In Myself By:

Today I Will Invest In Others By: My Previous Breakthrough Taught Me:

The Breakthrough I Received Today: The Miracle That Happened Today:

BREAKTHROUGHS AND MIRACLES

Today: Mood:

Today I Am Grateful For: Today's Prayer:

Today I Believe: Today I Am Making My Life Simple And
                                                Light By:

Today's Daydream: I Am Obeying The Spirit Within Me And
                                                Will Take Action On:

I Know I Am Not Limited To: Today I Will Invest In Myself By:

Today I Will Invest In Others By: My Previous Breakthrough Taught Me:

The Breakthrough I Received Today: The Miracle That Happened Today:

BREAKTHROUGHS AND MIRACLES

Today:

Today I Am Grateful For:

Today I Believe:

Today's Daydream:

I Know I Am Not Limited To:

Today I Will Invest In Others By:

The Breakthrough I Received Today:

Mood:

Today's Prayer:

Today I Am Making My Life Simple And Light By:

I Am Obeying The Spirit Within Me And Will Take Action On:

Today I Will Invest In Myself By:

My Previous Breakthrough Taught Me:

The Miracle That Happened Today:

But seek first his kingdom and his righteousness, and all these things will be given to you as well. Matthew 6:33

BREAKTHROUGHS AND MIRACLES

Today: Mood:

Today I Am Grateful For: Today's Prayer:

Today I Believe: Today I Am Making My Life Simple And
                                                    Light By:

Today's Daydream: I Am Obeying The Spirit Within Me And
                                                    Will Take Action On:

I Know I Am Not Limited To: Today I Will Invest In Myself By:

Today I Will Invest In Others By: My Previous Breakthrough Taught Me:

The Breakthrough I Received Today: The Miracle That Happened Today:

BREAKTHROUGHS AND MIRACLES

Today:

Today I Am Grateful For:

Today I Believe:

Today's Daydream:

I Know I Am Not Limited To:

Today I Will Invest In Others By:

The Breakthrough I Received Today:

Mood:

Today's Prayer:

Today I Am Making My Life Simple And Light By:

I Am Obeying The Spirit Within Me And Will Take Action On:

Today I Will Invest In Myself By:

My Previous Breakthrough Taught Me:

The Miracle That Happened Today:

SPIRITUAL NOTES

BREAKTHROUGHS AND MIRACLES

Today: Mood:

Today I Am Grateful For: Today's Prayer:

Today I Believe: Today I Am Making My Life Simple And
                                        Light By:

Today's Daydream: I Am Obeying The Spirit Within Me And
                                        Will Take Action On:

I Know I Am Not Limited To: Today I Will Invest In Myself By:

Today I Will Invest In Others By: My Previous Breakthrough Taught Me:

The Breakthrough I Received Today: The Miracle That Happened Today:

May the God of hope fill you with all joy and peace as you trust in him, so that you may overflow with hope by the power of the Holy Spirit.
Romans 15:13

BREAKTHROUGHS AND MIRACLES

Today:

Mood:

Today I Am Grateful For:

Today's Prayer:

Today I Believe:

Today I Am Making My Life Simple And Light By:

Today's Daydream:

I Am Obeying The Spirit Within Me And Will Take Action On:

I Know I Am Not Limited To:

Today I Will Invest In Myself By:

Today I Will Invest In Others By:

My Previous Breakthrough Taught Me:

The Breakthrough I Received Today:

The Miracle That Happened Today:

FEAR NOT, FOR I AM WITH

YOU;

be not dismayed, for I am your God; I
will strengthen you, I will help you, I
will uphold you with
my righteous right hand.

Isaiah 41:10

INVEST

In That Miracle You Are
Asking For.

BREAKTHROUGHS AND MIRACLES

Today:

Today I Am Grateful For:

Today I Believe:

Today's Daydream:

I Know I Am Not Limited To:

Today I Will Invest In Others By:

The Breakthrough I Received Today:

Mood:

Today's Prayer:

Today I Am Making My Life Simple And Light By:

I Am Obeying The Spirit Within Me And Will Take Action On:

Today I Will Invest In Myself By:

My Previous Breakthrough Taught Me:

The Miracle That Happened Today:

BREAKTHROUGHS AND MIRACLES

Today:

Today I Am Grateful For:

Today I Believe:

Today's Daydream:

I Know I Am Not Limited To:

Today I Will Invest In Others By:

The Breakthrough I Received Today:

Mood:

Today's Prayer:

Today I Am Making My Life Simple And Light By:

I Am Obeying The Spirit Within Me And Will Take Action On:

Today I Will Invest In Myself By:

My Previous Breakthrough Taught Me:

The Miracle That Happened Today:

BREAKTHROUGHS AND MIRACLES

Today:

Today I Am Grateful For:

Today I Believe:

Today's Daydream:

I Know I Am Not Limited To:

Today I Will Invest In Others By:

The Breakthrough I Received Today:

Mood:

Today's Prayer:

Today I Am Making My Life Simple And Light By:

I Am Obeying The Spirit Within Me And Will Take Action On:

Today I Will Invest In Myself By:

My Previous Breakthrough Taught Me:

The Miracle That Happened Today:

For I delight in loyalty rather than sacrifice, And in the knowledge of God rather than burnt offerings. Hosea 6:6

SPIRITUAL ACTION:

GIVE WHAT YOU WANT TO GET. YOU
WANT LOVE? GIVE IT. YOU WANT
MONEY? GIVE IT. YOU WANT A JOB?
GIVE IT. FEED OTHERS IN ORDER
TO BE FED.

YOUR BREAKTHROUGH
IS NOT ATTACHED TO THE
ONES WHO TRIED TO BREAK

BREAKTHROUGHS AND MIRACLES

Today:

Mood:

Today I Am Grateful For:

Today's Prayer:

Today I Believe:

Today I Am Making My Life Simple And Light By:

Today's Daydream:

I Am Obeying The Spirit Within Me And Will Take Action On:

I Know I Am Not Limited To:

Today I Will Invest In Myself By:

Today I Will Invest In Others By:

My Previous Breakthrough Taught Me:

The Breakthrough I Received Today:

The Miracle That Happened Today:

MY LOVE LETTER TO MY CURRENT BREAKTHROUGH AND MIRACLE

BREAKTHROUGHS AND MIRACLES

Today: Mood:

Today I Am Grateful For: Today's Prayer:

Today I Believe: Today I Am Making My Life Simple And
                                          Light By:

Today's Daydream: I Am Obeying The Spirit Within Me And
                                          Will Take Action On:

I Know I Am Not Limited To: Today I Will Invest In Myself By:

Today I Will Invest In Others By: My Previous Breakthrough Taught Me:

The Breakthrough I Received Today: The Miracle That Happened Today:

I am the good shepherd, and I know My own and I know My own and My own know Me John 10:14

BREAKTHROUGHS AND MIRACLES

Today:

Mood:

Today I Am Grateful For:

Today's Prayer:

Today I Believe:

Today I Am Making My Life Simple And Light By:

Today's Daydream:

I Am Obeying The Spirit Within Me And Will Take Action On:

I Know I Am Not Limited To:

Today I Will Invest In Myself By:

Today I Will Invest In Others By:

My Previous Breakthrough Taught Me:

The Breakthrough I Received Today:

The Miracle That Happened Today:

BREAKTHROUGHS AND MIRACLES

Today:

Today I Am Grateful For:

Today I Believe:

Today's Daydream:

I Know I Am Not Limited To:

Today I Will Invest In Others By:

The Breakthrough I Received Today:

Mood:

Today's Prayer:

Today I Am Making My Life Simple And Light By:

I Am Obeying The Spirit Within Me And Will Take Action On:

Today I Will Invest In Myself By:

My Previous Breakthrough Taught Me:

The Miracle That Happened Today:

FOR THE SPIRIT

GOD

gave us does not make us timid, but
gives us power, love and self-discipline.
2 Timonthy 1:7

BREAKTHROUGHS AND MIRACLES

Today:

Mood:

Today I Am Grateful For:

Today's Prayer:

Today I Believe:

Today I Am Making My Life Simple And Light By:

Today's Daydream:

I Am Obeying The Spirit Within Me And Will Take Action On:

I Know I Am Not Limited To:

Today I Will Invest In Myself By:

Today I Will Invest In Others By:

My Previous Breakthrough Taught Me:

The Breakthrough I Received Today:

The Miracle That Happened Today:

Teach me good discernment and knowledge, For I believe in Your commandments. Psalm 119:66

BREAKTHROUGHS AND MIRACLES

Today:

Today I Am Grateful For:

Today I Believe:

Today's Daydream:

I Know I Am Not Limited To:

Today I Will Invest In Others By:

The Breakthrough I Received Today:

Mood:

Today's Prayer:

Today I Am Making My Life Simple And Light By:

I Am Obeying The Spirit Within Me And Will Take Action On:

Today I Will Invest In Myself By:

My Previous Breakthrough Taught Me:

The Miracle That Happened Today:

I WILL

NEVER
GIVE UP

On What I Believe. Never.

BREAKTHROUGHS AND MIRACLES

Today: Mood:

Today I Am Grateful For: Today's Prayer:

Today I Believe: Today I Am Making My Life Simple And
                                        Light By:

Today's Daydream: I Am Obeying The Spirit Within Me And
                                        Will Take Action On:

I Know I Am Not Limited To: Today I Will Invest In Myself By:

Today I Will Invest In Others By: My Previous Breakthrough Taught Me:

The Breakthrough I Received Today: The Miracle That Happened Today:

He must increase, but I must decrease. John 3:30

BREAKTHROUGHS AND MIRACLES

Today:

Mood:

Today I Am Grateful For:

Today's Prayer:

Today I Believe:

Today I Am Making My Life Simple And Light By:

Today's Daydream:

I Am Obeying The Spirit Within Me And Will Take Action On:

I Know I Am Not Limited To:

Today I Will Invest In Myself By:

Today I Will Invest In Others By:

My Previous Breakthrough Taught Me:

The Breakthrough I Received Today:

The Miracle That Happened Today:

THROUGH IT ALL, A WAY IS ALWAYS

CREATED
BECAUSE
I BELIEVE.

What May Have Hurt Me Has
Made Me Stronger And Created A
Breakthrough For My Next Miracle.
I Relax Knowing That God's Love
Protects Me And Grows Me.
Life Just Keeps
Getting Better.

Made in the
USA
Middletown, DE

76957716R00150